ABOLITIONISTS

"Every slave is a stolen man;
every slaveholder is a man stealer."
～ William Lloyd Garrison ～

BY SARAH E. DE CAPUA

The Child's World®
childsworld.com

Published by The Child's World®
1980 Lookout Drive • Mankato, MN 56003-1705
800-599-READ • www.childsworld.com

PHOTOS

Cover and page 4: Everett Collection/Shutterstock.com
Interior:AP Photo/The Daily Journal, Dennis Reavis: 17; Bettmann via Getty Images:
18; Collection of the Smithsonian National Museum of African American History
and Culture, Gift from the Liljenquist Family Collection: 6, 20; Collection of the
Smithsonian National Museum of African American History and Culture, Gift of Joele
and Fred Michaud: 22; Everett Collection/Newscom: 16; F. Smith & Son (Portland,
ME)/Library of Congress, Prints and Photographs Division: 10, 29 (left); Ken Welsh/
ZUMA Press/Newscom: 8; National Portrait Gallery, Smithsonian Institution, Gift
of Marliese R. and Sylvester G. March: 12; National Portrait Gallery, Smithsonian
Institution: 9, 11, 23, 27, 31; North Wind Picture Archives: 5, 7, 24, 25, 26, 29 (right);
Picture History/Newscom: 15; Schomburg Center for Research in Black Culture,
Manuscripts, Archives, and Rare Books Division, The New York Public Library: 13, 19,
21; The Metropolitan Museum of Art, Gift of Mr. and Mrs. Carl Stoeckel, 1897: 14

LIBRARY OF CONGRESS CATALOGING-IN-PUBLICATION DATA
ISBN 9781503854406 (Reinforced Library Binding)
ISBN 9781503854864 (Portable Document Format)
ISBN 9781503855243 (Online Multi-user eBook)
LCCN: 2021930422

Printed in the United States of America

Cover and page 4 caption:
This woodcut from the 1780s shows an enslaved man pleading for compassion. The illustration was originally used by abolitionists in Great Britain.

CONTENTS

AM I NOT A MAN AND A BROTHER?

Chapter One

SLAVERY IN THE UNITED STATES

"Neither slavery nor **involuntary servitude***…shall exist within the United States…."*

These words are from the Thirteenth **Amendment** to the United States Constitution. The amendment was ratified, or officially agreed upon, by the U.S. **Congress** on December 6, 1865. The amendment ended slavery in the United States forever.

These words, however, were not just an addition to the Constitution, the document that gives us the principles by which the United States is governed. They marked the end of a long struggle for freedom waged by Black Americans and white Americans on behalf of enslaved people. The struggle lasted more than 200 years and was one of the reasons for the American Civil War (1861–1865).

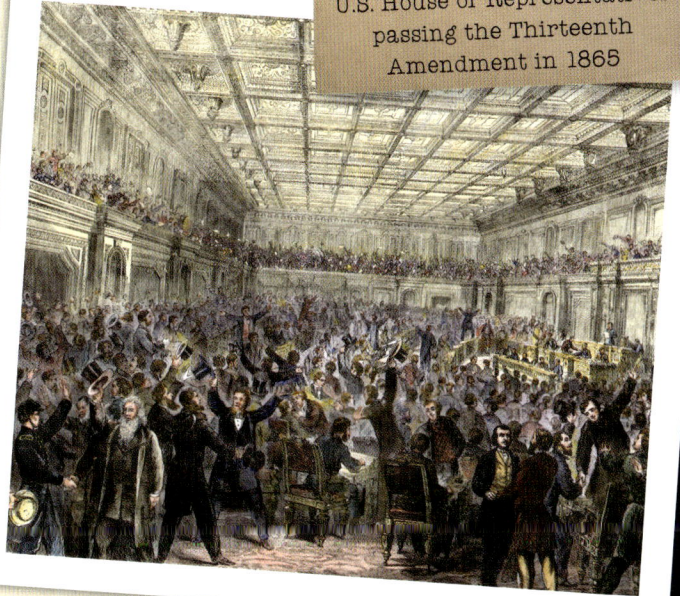

U.S. House of Representatives passing the Thirteenth Amendment in 1865

Public Sale.

Will be sold to the highest bidder for cash in hand, on

Tuesday the 14th day of June,

At Robard's & Curd's Store, about 3 miles from the mouth of Dick's river, Mercer county, Six or Eight likely NEGROES, to satisfy a decree or judgment of the Jessamine circuit court.

BEN. BRADSHAW,

Exe'r. of B. BRADSHAW, Dec'd. and Agent for Curd's Heirs.

June 6th 1836.

An announcement for the sale of enslaved people in Kentucky.

The first Black people who arrived in what was to become the United States did so in the 1600s as **indentured servants**. They pledged to work for the person or family who paid their way across the ocean for a period of about seven years. When the agreed upon number of years was completed, most freed servants took their places in their communities. They became respected, contributing members of society.

By the end of the 1600s, indentured servitude was no longer a choice, however. Black people from Africa and the Caribbean were kidnapped, chained, and brought to the **colonies** as unwilling servants and laborers for white settlers in the North and the South.

By the early 1800s, slavery had nearly ended in the northern United States. As the region's **economy** grew to depend on manufacturing, the labor of farm workers became less necessary. The number of Black people living in the north, free or enslaved, was less than 60,000—a fraction of the white population. And laws were being written in nearly every northern state to abolish, or permanently end, slavery altogether.

Around 10 million to 12 million Africans were kidnapped and forced into the slave trade. The journey on slave ships across the Atlantic Ocean, known as the Middle Passage, was treacherous. Enslaved Africans were chained together and forced into cramped, overcrowded spaces below the ship's deck. Many died from sickness and the inhumane living conditions.

The agricultural economy in the South, however, was almost totally dependent on the labor of enslaved people. By 1860, when the total U.S. population was 31 million, almost 4 million enslaved people lived in the South. Southern enslavers insisted that forced labor was a normal way of life. They argued that if slavery were abolished, the South's economy would be ruined.

Enslaved workers unloading rice barges in South Carolina.

7

As Americans in the North and the South struggled over the legal right to own enslaved people, groups of people called **abolitionists** focused on the **moral** right to own other people. Since before the country's beginnings, when it was just a loosely knit collection of colonies, abolitionists had insisted that it was **immoral** for one human being to own another. Their goal was to end slavery in the United States forever.

The first people to speak out forcefully in favor of abolishing slavery were members of the Religious Order of the Society of Friends, also known as Quakers. The religion's founder, George Fox, began speaking of abolition in the mid-1600s. The Quakers stressed that slavery was a violation of God's law. In the years that saw the struggle for freedom for all Americans, abolitionists found a variety of ways to spread their message. These methods included individuals who spoke to audiences of supporters; newspapers and organizations that advanced the cause; and the **Underground Railroad**, which helped enslaved people escape.

George Fox preaching to a crowd in Maryland in 1671.

Chapter Two

INSPIRING INDIVIDUALS

Many people—Black and white, men and women—spoke out **eloquently** against slavery. Perhaps the best remembered are those who dedicated their lives to the abolitionist cause during the late 1700s and 1800s. Some of the best-known abolitionists were themselves formerly enslaved. Richard Allen, Sojourner Truth, Frederick Douglass, and Harriet Tubman spoke of their experiences as enslaved people to help audiences understand the injustices that they, and other formerly enslaved people, faced.

Richard Allen (1760–1831) was born into slavery in Philadelphia. In 1780, he paid his enslaver $2,000 for his own freedom. Allen spent his years as a free man working and preaching. He became a Methodist minister in 1782, and began preaching at Philadelphia's

Richard Allen

St. George's Methodist Church in 1786. Soon after, Allen founded the Free African Society. The society worked to provide spiritual guidance, education, and health care to Black people.

In 1816, Allen helped establish the African Methodist Episcopal (AME) Church. Allen believed that Black members of society should have their own church in which to worship. Today, African Methodist Episcopal churches can be found throughout the United States.

Sojourner Truth (1797?–1883) was freed from slavery when the state of New York passed an **emancipation** law that became effective on July 4, 1827. Deeply religious, Truth was at first a preacher. By 1851, she was a popular speaker at abolitionist **conventions** in New England. Another abolitionist, William Lloyd Garrison, had convinced her to join him on a lecture tour. As an enslaved person, she did not learn to read or write, so she **dictated** her **autobiography**, called *Narrative of Sojourner Truth,* to a friend in 1850. She believed in using nonviolent methods to end slavery.

Frederick Douglass (1818–1895) was a fugitive who became the most famous Black man of his day, as well as one of the most popular speakers in the abolitionist movement. He published three autobiographies, *Narrative of the Life of Frederick Douglass, My Bondage and My Freedom*, and *The Life and Times of Frederick Douglass*. Douglass also published his own antislavery newspaper, the *North Star*.

Frederick Douglass in 1864

Harriet Tubman (1820–1913) is known as the Moses of her people. Like the biblical Moses who led the Israelites out of slavery in Egypt, Tubman led Black people out of slavery in the South. She escaped from slavery in 1849 and spent the following ten years guiding more than 300 enslaved people to freedom on the Underground Railroad. After the Civil War (1861–1865), Tubman spent the rest of her life speaking out about these experiences and supporting other important issues, such as women's rights.

Many abolitionists were neither Black nor formerly enslaved people. A well known white abolitionist, William Lloyd Garrison (1805–1879), was born in Massachusetts. He was indentured at age 14 to a newspaper printer. As a result, he became an expert printer. Throughout Garrison's childhood, he was troubled by the enslavement of Black people. As he grew older, he wrote countless articles calling slavery immoral. These articles helped to influence people in the North to abolish slavery.

In addition to leading enslaved people to freedom on the Underground Railroad, Harriet Tubman served in the Union army during the Civil War. Her knowledge of the land and her ability to travel in secret made her a good spy and scout. She also served as a nurse, tending to sick and wounded Union soldiers. When Tubman died in 1913, she was buried with military honors.

Harriet Tubman in 1885.

Some abolitionists believed in freeing enslaved people gradually over time. Garrison believed in complete and immediate freedom for all enslaved workers. He became a prominent spokesman for the abolitionist cause and was a featured speaker at conventions throughout the North. Garrison also established newspapers and organizations to help further abolition.

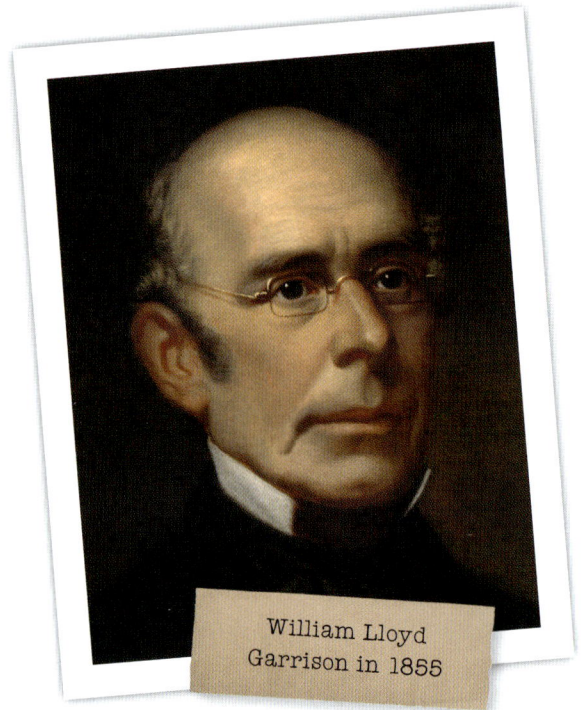

Some abolitionists did not believe in ending slavery by peaceful methods, or by escaping when possible. They believed in using force when necessary, and they encouraged enslaved people to rebel against their enslavers. Nat Turner and John Brown led famous **revolts**. Though unsuccessful, the revolts shed light on the urgent need many Americans felt to free enslaved people.

Nat Turner (1800–1831) became the most feared enslaved person in America after he led a failed revolt in Virginia. The uprising began at midnight on August 22, 1831, when Turner and four of his followers killed six people on his enslaver's farm. The dead included Turner's enslaver, Joseph Travis, and Travis's wife.

William Lloyd Garrison in 1855

After Nat Turner was captured, a white man named Thomas R. Gray interviewed him while he was imprisoned. Gray published Turner's story in 1831 as The Confessions of Nat Turner. Turner was very religious. When he saw a solar eclipse, he considered it a sign from God to revolt against the evils of slavery. "I should arise and prepare myself," Turner said, "and slay my enemies with their own weapons."

Turner and his followers then stole horses and rode from farm to farm, where they were joined by more enslaved people. By the following day, 60 workers had joined the rebellion. By the time authorities crushed the rebellion late in the day on August 23, at least 57 white people, including women and infants, had been killed.

For more than two months, Turner hid in the woods to avoid capture. He was finally caught on October 30, 1831. He stood trial for the **insurrection** on November 5. When the trial was over, Turner was found guilty and sentenced to death. He was hanged on November 11, 1831. Twenty other rebels were hanged as well. The result of Turner's failed revolt was harsher treatment of enslaved people by their enslavers, who feared that their workers, too, would rise up against them. In spite of this harsher treatment, many enslaved people and free Black people saw Nat Turner as a hero. Later abolitionists considered him to be a **martyr** to their cause.

Nat Turner and other enslaved men planning their revolt.

13

John Brown (1800–1859), a white man, was born and raised in Connecticut. In 1849, Brown and his family settled in the Black community of North Elba, New York. Brown hated slavery and believed God was telling him to free every enslaved person. In 1859, Brown devised a plan to capture the federal **arsenal** at Harpers Ferry, Virginia. He would give the guns stored there to enslaved workers so they could fight for their freedom. Brown told his friend, Frederick Douglass, about the plan. Douglass tried unsuccessfully to convince Brown that the plan would not work.

John Brown kisses a baby as he is taken to be hanged in 1859.

Brown's raid on Harpers Ferry began on October 16, 1859, when he led a band of 18 men to seize the arsenal. They succeeded, but a two-day standoff with U.S. Marines led to the death of two of Brown's sons. Brown was captured, tried, and convicted of **treason**, insurrection, and murder. (A railroad guard on a bridge to Harpers Ferry was killed by one of Brown's men, and a wounded marine later died.) Brown was sentenced to death and hanged on December 2, 1859. Harriet Tubman mourned his loss, calling him the "Savior of our People."

Henry Highland Garnet (1815–1882) was born enslaved in Maryland. When he was 9 years old, his enslaver died and Garnet's father began planning the family's escape to freedom in the North. The family traveled along the Underground Railroad until they reached New York City. In 1842, Garnet became a minister. He used his sermons to preach about the evils of slavery and shared his ideas about what his fellow Black people could do to help end it. He also wrote newspaper articles that reflected his opinions.

Garnet believed slavery would not end without violence and political action. He urged enslaved people to kill their enslavers. He delivered a famous speech at the 1843 National Negro Convention in Buffalo, New York.

Henry Highland Garnet

In it, he urged enslaved workers everywhere to resist their **oppressors**. Garnet insisted that it was better to "die freemen than live to be slaves." After the passage of the Thirteenth Amendment, Garnet's work to support abolition shifted to achieving equality for Black people.

Other individuals who devoted themselves to the cause of ending slavery in the United States included Mary Ann Shadd Cary, Wendell Phillips, Maria Stewart, and William Still.

Chapter Three

THE UNDERGROUND RAILROAD

Legend tells of a fugitive worker named Tice Davids, who escaped from his enslaver's Kentucky farm in 1831. With his enslaver pursuing him in order to recapture him, Davids swam across the Ohio River. He emerged from the river in the town of Ripley. Ripley was located in Ohio, a **Free State**. A white man who lived in the town hid Davids in his basement.

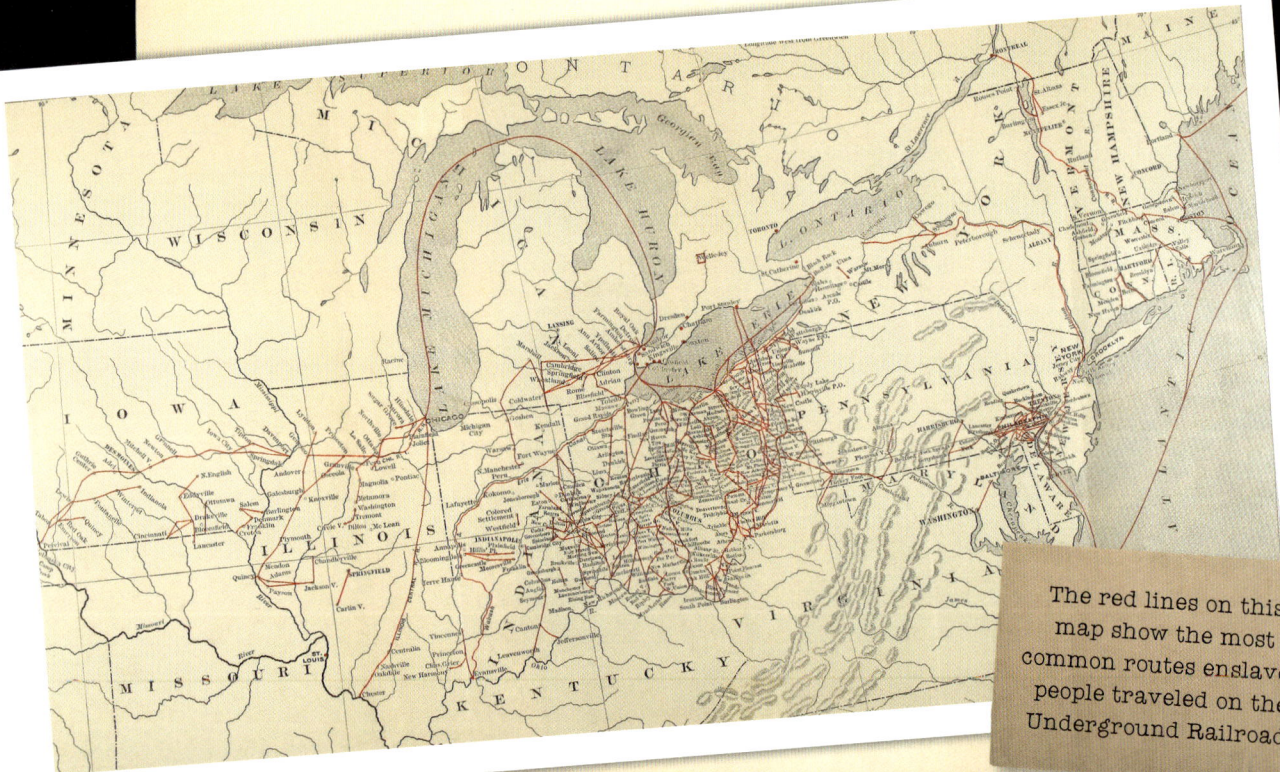

The red lines on this map show the most common routes enslaved people traveled on the Underground Railroad.

Davids's enslaver searched the town for hours. He finally gave up, saying, "Davids must have gone off on some underground railroad." This is the first time the term "underground railroad" was used. It was not a real railroad, but the people involved in it used railroad terms. Houses where the **fugitives** from slavery were hidden were called "stations." The owners of the houses were called "stationmasters." Guides were called "conductors." The fugitives were called "passengers."

It was against the law to help enslaved people who were trying to escape, so there was no single leader of the Underground Railroad. Stations were kept secret. Most members of the Underground Railroad did not know each other, but their goal was to abolish slavery in the United States. While many worked by day to achieve that goal, all worked by night to take fugitives into their homes. They hid the enslaved people in their basements, their attics, or in secret passageways of their homes. Other hiding places included rooms with removable floorboards, wagons with false bottoms, and barns with hidden basements. Fugitives could rest in these hiding places. Stationmasters gave the fugitives food and other supplies. When it was time for the fugitives to move on to the next station, they traveled north to the Free States and to Canada.

This house in Wilmington, Illinois was a station on the Underground Railroad. It is thought that the small area at the top of the house was used to signal fugitives, alerting them that the home was safe.

Both Black and white people worked together to help fugitives on the Underground Railroad. The Indiana home of Levi Coffin and his wife, Catherine, is today one of the best-known stations on the Underground Railroad. Over many years, thousands of fugitives from slavery found safety in the Coffin house.

> The Coffin house was called the "Grand Central Station" of the Underground Railroad. Three of the routes met at the location, and thousands of fugitives sought safety there.

Thomas Garrett's home in Delaware also was an Underground Railroad station. During the years it served as a station, about 2,500 fugitives were hidden there. One of the fugitives was Harriet Tubman. Tubman went on to be a conductor on the Underground Railroad and guided more than 300 people to freedom.

Levi Coffin (blue coat and hat) and Catherine (red shawl) helping fugitives on the Underground Railroad

Lyman Beecher's home in Cincinnati, Ohio, was also a station. His daughter, Harriet Beecher Stowe, helped him. In 1852, Stowe published *Uncle Tom's Cabin*, the story of an enslaved Black woman who escapes from her enslaver with her baby. Readers of the book learned of the cruelty and injustice of slavery. The novel gave strength to the abolitionist movement and is still considered to be one of the causes of the Civil War.

William Still became known as the Father of the Underground Railroad. He helped hundreds of fugitives escape to freedom.

Frederick Douglass operated a station from his newspaper office in Rochester, New York. Many fugitives traveled through Douglass's station.

Jermain Loguen was another fugitive who served as a stationmaster. He hid about 1,500 people in his New York home.

William Still was a free Black man who lived in Philadelphia, Pennsylvania. Still worked on the Underground Railroad and, in spite of the danger of being caught, kept notes about his experiences. His notes were published in 1872 as a book called *The Underground Rail Road Records*. It is one of the most famous books ever published about the Underground Railroad.

Today, many houses on the Underground Railroad have been preserved and are now open as museums. Each year, thousands of visitors tour these former stations. Houses in states such as Ohio, Pennsylvania, Indiana, and Delaware are among those that continue to serve as reminders of the abolitionist movement.

Chapter Four

NEWSPAPERS CHAMPION THE CAUSE

Without radio or television, newspapers were the most significant means of keeping current with the important issues and events of life in the United States. The issue of slavery appeared often, especially in newspapers located in northern and southern cities.

Newspapers devoted to bringing the abolitionist cause to as many readers as possible sprang up throughout the North. They were read widely by both Black and white people.

In 1821, Benjamin Lundy began publishing the antislavery newspaper, the *Genius of Universal Emancipation*. Lundy, a Quaker living in Baltimore, Maryland, published the newspaper from 1821 to 1835. Lundy moved to Illinois in 1839 and once again began publishing the *Genius of Universal Emancipation*. He continued to publish it until his death later that same year.

This issue of the *Liberator* was from November 23, 1855.

William Lloyd Garrison published newspapers with the purpose of convincing enslavers that they were evil and that slavery was sinful. Garrison's best-known newspaper was the *Liberator*, which was published from 1831 to 1865. Frederick Douglass considered this newspaper second only to the Bible in its importance to his life.

FREEDOM'S JOURNAL.

BY JNO. B. RUSSWURM.
"RIGHTEOUSNESS EXALTETH A NATION."
NEW-YORK, FRIDAY, MARCH 14, 1828.
VOL. I.—NO. LI.

THE COLORED AMERICAN.

SAMUEL E. CORNISH,
Editor.

New-York, Saturday, May 13, 1837.

PHILIP A. BELL

Samuel Cornish (right) and another editor appeared in this 1837 issue of the *Colored American*.

A newspaper called the *Colored American* was established in 1837 and was edited by Samuel Cornish. The articles of Henry Highland Garnet, a free Black man committed to ending slavery, were often featured in the paper. The *Colored American* focused on abolitionist and slavery issues until 1841, its last year of publication.

The *National Anti-Slavery Standard* was a weekly newspaper published by Lydia Maria Child and her husband David. It was published in New York from 1841 to 1870.

The *North Star* was published in Rochester, New York, from 1847 to 1851 by Frederick Douglass. The first issue appeared on December 3, 1847. Douglass edited and published newspapers for the next 25 years. The *North Star* allowed him to further express his abolitionist views.

Frederick Douglass sits at his desk in 1879

The *Anti-Slavery Reporter* was published in New York City during the 1840s by the American and Foreign Anti-Slavery Society. The paper would accept cash contributions toward its expenses only from people who did not earn their money through slavery.

Among the many other antislavery newspapers were the *Free Enquirer, Pennsylvania Freeman*, and *Freedom's Journal*, the first newspaper in the United States published entirely by Black people. All of these papers sought to reach as many readers as possible with the plight of the enslaved.

The need for abolitionist newspapers ended with the passage of the Thirteenth Amendment. During the existence of these and other, smaller papers, however, they were an important voice for abolition.

Chapter Five

ABOLITIONISTS ORGANIZE

Since the beginning of slavery in America, people spoke out against it. As more and more people saw the injustice of slavery, they formed groups, or organizations, to make their views known publicly and to help bring attention to the abolitionist cause. Many small societies and organizations existed throughout the 1700s. In 1786, Benjamin Franklin became the first president of the Pennsylvania Society for Promoting the Abolition of Slavery. The best-known organizations, however, came into existence in the 50 years before the Civil War.

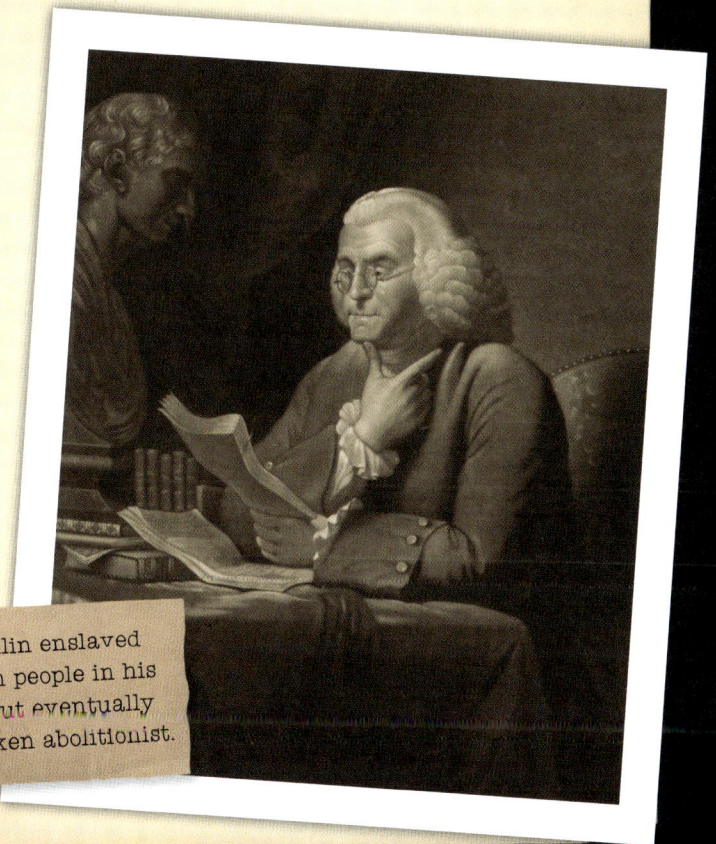

Benjamin Franklin enslaved as many as seven people in his younger years, but eventually became an outspoken abolitionist.

In 1816, the American Colonization Society was founded. Formed in Washington, DC, the society sought to provide money for the **emigration** of Black people to Africa. Members and supporters of the organization believed that Black people

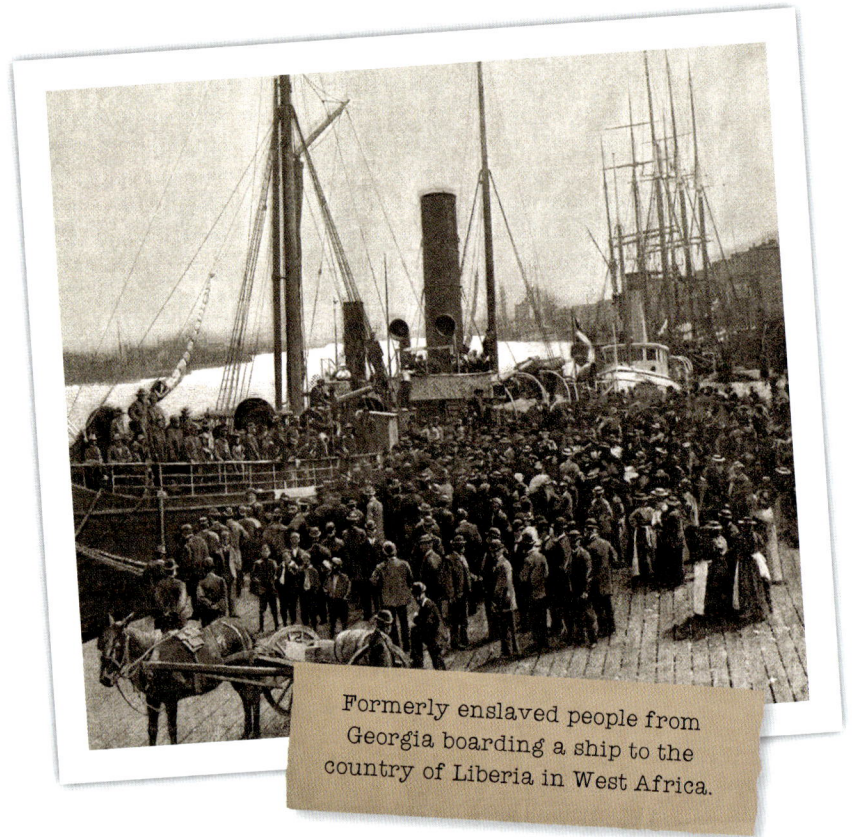

Formerly enslaved people from Georgia boarding a ship to the country of Liberia in West Africa.

brought to the United States, or their **descendants**, should be returned to Africa. The West African nation of Liberia was established by the American Colonization Society in 1822 as a permanent home for people formerly enslaved in the United States.

The American Society of Free Persons of Color was founded in Philadelphia, Pennsylvania, in 1830. It was formed to oppose the work of the American Colonization Society. The society's members focused on abolishing slavery and making life better for free men and women in the United States. It also made plans to establish a community in Canada for Black people who wanted to escape discrimination in the United States.

William Lloyd Garrison, the publisher of the *Liberator*, founded the American Anti-Slavery Society in Massachusetts in 1833. Garrison and his followers in the organization (often called Garrisonians) believed in abolishing slavery through persuasion, convincing enslavers that their practices were morally wrong. The American Anti-Slavery Society encouraged lectures and the publication of newspapers and other printed materials to achieve that goal. Members did not believe that political measures would bring about the end of slavery.

The American and Foreign Anti-Slavery Society was formed in 1840. Founded by Arthur and Lewis Tappan in Rochester, New York, it was made up of former members of Garrison's American Anti-Slavery Society.

Pro-slavery rioters burn an abolitionist's shop in Illinois.

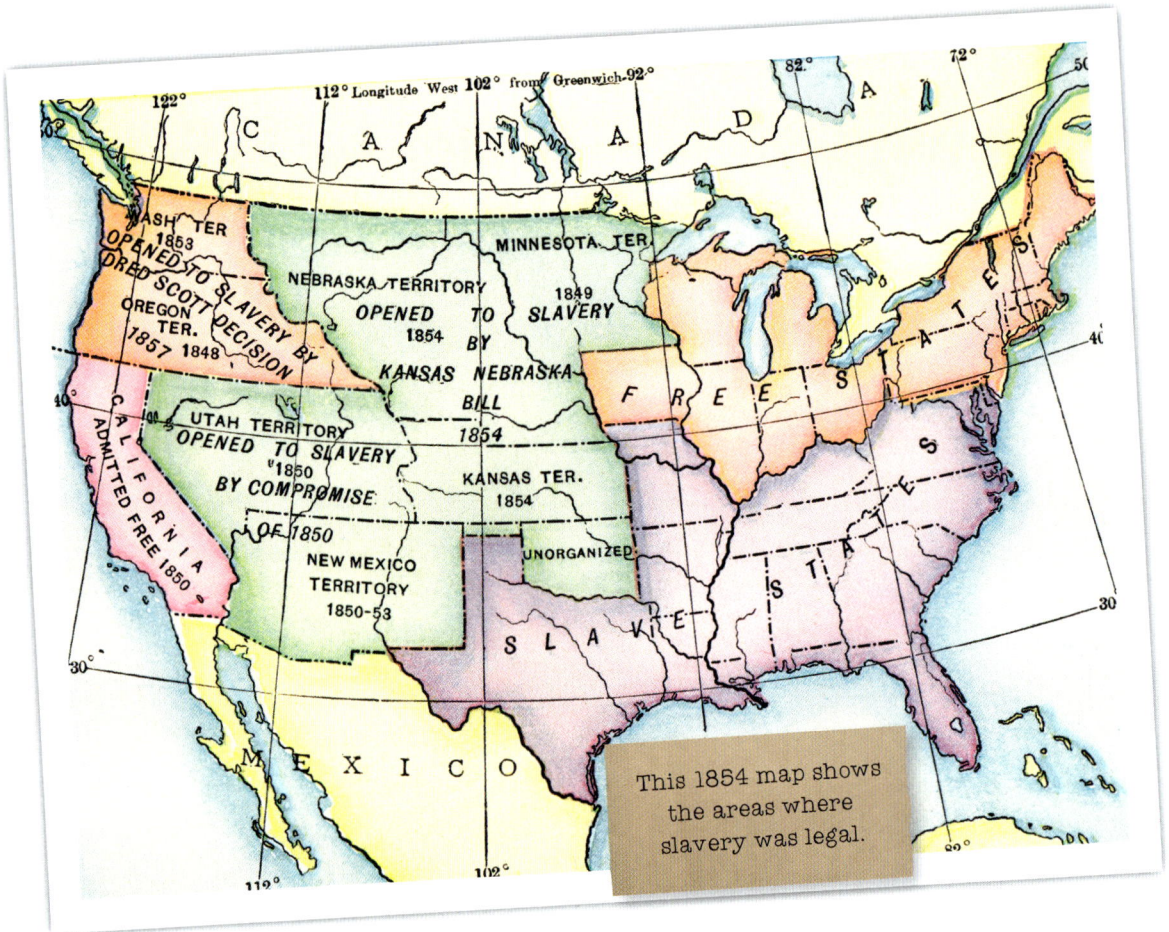

This 1854 map shows the areas where slavery was legal.

In 1858, the African Civilization Society was founded by Henry Highland Garnet, who founded the *Colored American* newspaper, and another Black leader, Martin Delany. Based in New York City, the society hoped to end slavery by encouraging Black people to resettle in Africa, where they could grow cotton. Members of the African Civilization Society argued that the competition with the South's most important and profitable crop, which was also cotton, would eventually end the need for slavery in the South.

Major cities in the North also established their own antislavery societies. Such cities included Philadelphia, New York, and Boston. By the end of the 1850s, in spite of the efforts of abolitionist individuals, groups, and publications—or perhaps because of them—it became clear that the United States was heading for an actual battle against slavery. It took the Civil War, the **Emancipation Proclamation** of 1863, and the Thirteenth Amendment to accomplish what many abolitionists had spent their lives trying to achieve.

The Emancipation Proclamation was the first step toward the abolition of slavery in America. After President Lincoln issued the proclamation, many enslaved people fled to northern states or even to Union army camps seeking freedom. Thousands ended up joining the fight. Over the course of the Civil War, about 200,000 Black Americans served in the Union army.

President Abraham Lincoln (third from left) signing the Emancipation Proclamation on January 1, 1863. This law freed enslaved people in the rebelling states during the Civil War.

Many abolitionists were white.
Why is it important that white people
joined in the cause to help abolish slavery?

**More than 30,000 people are said to have
escaped slavery via the Underground Railroad.**
If there was no Underground Railroad, what would have
happened to enslaved people who wanted to escape?
What would you have done if you were an enslaved worker in the 1860?

TIME LINE

1600-1799

1600s
The first Black people arrive as indentured servants in what is now the United States.

1700
Slavery is an established institution in the North and the South.

1760
Richard Allen is born enslaved in Philadelphia.

1786
Benjamin Franklin becomes the first president of the Pennsylvania Society for Promoting the Abolition of Slavery.

ca. 1797
Sojourner Truth is born into slavery in New York.

1800-1819

1800s
Slavery ends in the North.

1800
Nat Turner is born enslaved in Virginia. John Brown is born in Connecticut.

1805
William Lloyd Garrison is born in Massachusetts.

1815
Henry Highland Garnet is born into slavery in Maryland.

1816
Richard Allen helps to establish the African Methodist Episcopal (AME) Church. The American Colonization Society is founded.

1818
Frederick Douglass is born into slavery in Maryland.

1820-1839

1820
Harriet Tubman is born enslaved in Maryland.

1821
Benjamin Lundy begins publishing *Genius of Universal Emancipation*.

1827
New York abolishes slavery.

1830
The American Society of Free Persons of Color is founded.

1831
Nat Turner leads an unsuccessful rebellion in Virginia on August 22. Garrison begins publishing the *Liberator*.

1833
Garrison founds the American Anti-Slavery Society.

1837
The *Colored American* newspaper is established.

**This book discusses many abolitionists who wrote
and spoke about the horrors of enslavement.**
How does spreading information about slavery help to end it?

**Abolitionists had lots of ideas for ways to end slavery in America.
Henry Highland Garnet wanted Black people to resettle in Africa
and grow cotton there. By doing so, he hoped it would end
the need for slavery in the South.**
What are the strengths and weaknesses of his idea?
Looking back, what do you think was the best way to end slavery?

1840

1840s
The *Anti-Slavery Reporter* is
published in New York City.

1840
Arthur and Lewis Tappan
establish the American and
Foreign Anti-Slavery Society.

1841
The National Anti-Slavery
Standard is published in New York.

1843
Henry Highland Garnet speaks
at the National Negro Convention
in Buffalo, New York.

1847
Frederick Douglass begins
publishing the *North Star*.

1850

1858
The African Civilization Society
is established.

1859
John Brown's raid on Harpers
Ferry, Virginia, begins on
October 16.

1860

1861
The Civil War begins.

1863
President Abraham Lincoln issues
the Emancipation Proclamation
on January 1.

1865
The Civil War ends. The Thirteenth
Amendment to the Constitution
is ratified.

abolitionists (ab-uh-LISH-un-ists)
Abolitionists were people who worked to abolish slavery before the Civil War. Frederick Douglass and William Lloyd Garrison were famous abolitionists.

amendment (uh-MEND-munt)
An amendment is a change that is made to a law or legal document. Congress had to pass amendments to the Constitution to end slavery.

arsenal (AHR-suh-nuhl)
An arsenal is a storage place for weapons and ammunition.

autobiography (aw-toh-by-OG-ruh-fee)
An autobiography is a book in which the author tells the story of his or her life.

colonies (KOL-uh-neez)
Colonies are territories controlled by another country.

Congress (KONG-griss)
Congress is the U.S. government body that makes laws. It is made up of the House of Representatives and the Senate.

conventions (kuhn-VEN-shuhns)
Conventions are large gatherings of people who have the same interests.

descendants (di-SEND-uhnts)
Descendants are someone's children, grandchildren, and so on.

dictated (DIK-tay-ted)
To dictate something is to say it aloud while another person writes it down. Sojourner Truth could neither read nor write, so she dictated her autobiography to a friend.

economy (ee-KON-uh-mee)
An economy is the way a country or state runs its industry, trade, or finance.

eloquently (EL-uh-kwuhnt-lee)
Someone who speaks eloquently has a smooth, clear voice.

emancipation (i-man-si-PAY-shuhn)
Emancipation is the act of freeing a person or group from slavery or control.

Emancipation Proclamation (i-man-si-PAY-shuhn prok-luh-MAY-shuhn)
The Emancipation Proclamation is the law signed by President Abraham Lincoln on January 1, 1863, that freed enslaved people in the rebelling states.

emigration (em-uh-GRAY-shuhn)
Emigration is the act of leaving one country in order to live permanently in another.

Free State (FREE STAYT)
A Free State was a state in which slavery was legal before 1865.

fugitives (ih-MOR-ullz)
People who are running away, especially from the law, are fugitives. Enslaved workers who escaped from slavery were fugitives.

immoral (ih-MOR-ull)
An immoral person has no sense of right and wrong.

indentured servants (in-DEN-churd SUR-vuhnts)
Indentured servants are people who sign a contract to work for a certain period of time in return for payment of travel expenses.

insurrection (in-suh-REK-shuhn)
An insurrection is a revolt against a government. Nat Turner led an insurrection.

involuntary servitude (in-VOL-uhn-ter-ee SER-vuh-tood)
A person in involuntary servitude is denied the freedom to make his or her own choices.

martyr (MAR-tur)
A martyr is someone who is killed or made to suffer because of his or her beliefs.

moral (MOR-ull)
A moral person is able to distinguish right from wrong.

oppressors (uh-PRESS-uhrs)
Oppressors are people who are cruel to others.

revolts (reh-VOLTS)
A revolt is a rebellion against a government or an authority. Nat Turner led a famous revolt in Virginia.

scout (SKAOWT)
A scout is a person who is sent to find out information Harriet Tubman was a scout for the Union army.

treason (TREE-zun)
Treason is the crime of betraying one's country.

Underground Railroad (UHN-dur-ground RAYL-rohd)
The Underground Railroad was a collection of safe hiding places, usually the homes of abolitionists, for enslaved people escaping from the South to new homes in the Free Northern States or in Canada.

Union (YOON-yun)
During the U.S. Civil War, the northern states were called the Union. Harriet Tubman served in the Union army.

BOOKS

Maloof, Torrey. *Abolitionists: What We Need Is Action.* Huntington Beach, CA: Teacher Created Materials, 2017.

McDonough, Yona Zeldis. *What Was The Underground Railroad?* New York, NY: Grosset & Dunlap, 2013.

McNeese, Tim. *The Abolitionist Movement: Ending Slavery.* New York, NY: Chelsea House, 2008.

Morlock, Jeremy. *Abolitionists and Slave Owners.* New York, NY: PowerKids Press, 2020.

Tate, Don. *William Still and His Freedom Stories: The Father of the Underground Railroad.* Atlanta, GA: Peachtree Publishing, 2020.

WEBSITES

Visit our website for links about abolitionists:

childsworld.com/links

Note to Parents, Teachers, and Librarians: We routinely verify our Web links to make sure they are safe, active sites—so encourage your readers to check them out!

INDEX